PIANO VOCAL GUIT

NEIL DIAMOND
DREAMS

ISBN 978-1-61780-378-9

HAL•LEONARD®
CORPORATION
7777 W. BLUEMOUND RD. P.O. BOX 13819 MILWAUKEE, WI 53213

Visit Hal Leonard Online at
www.halleonard.com

AIN'T NO SUNSHINE

Words and Music by
BILL WITHERS

Ain't no sun - shine when she's gone. ___

It's not warm ___ when she's a - way. ___

Ain't no sun - shine when she's gone, ___ but she's al - ways gone ___ too long, ___

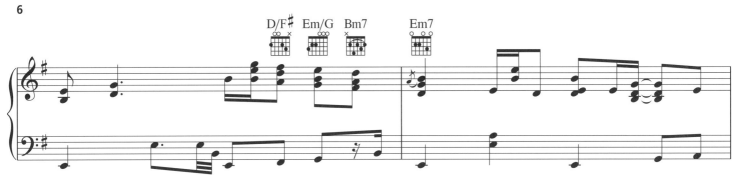

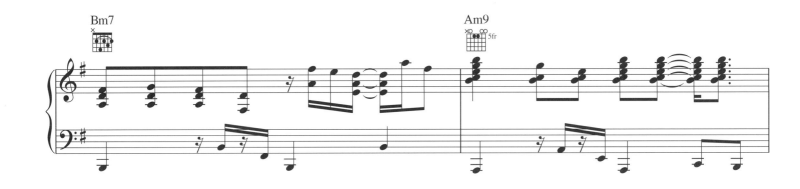

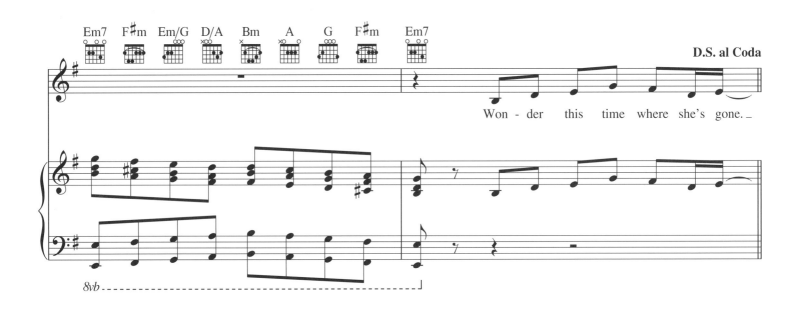

D.S. al Coda

Won - der this time where she's gone. _

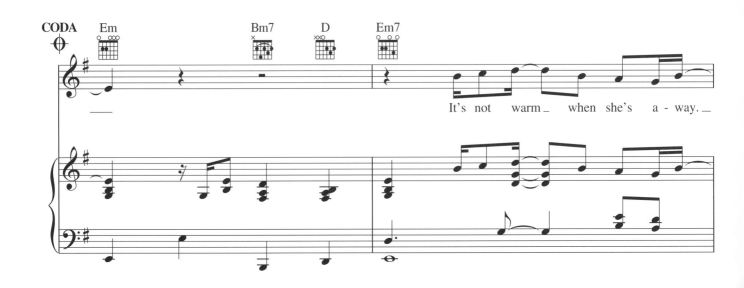

It's not warm _ when she's a - way. _

BLACKBIRD

Words and Music by JOHN LENNON
and PAUL McCARTNEY

ALONE AGAIN NATURALLY

Words and Music by
GILBERT O'SULLIVAN

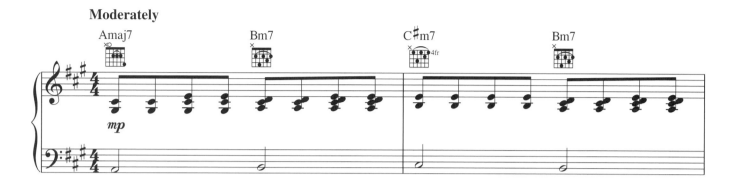

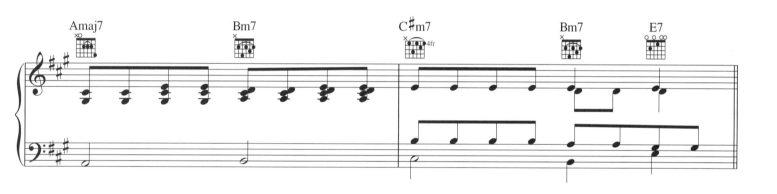

(1.) In a lit - tle while from now, __ if I'm not feel - in' an - y less sour, I

(D.S.) *Guitar solo ad lib.*

18

FEELS LIKE HOME

Words and Music by
RANDY NEWMAN

Additional lyrics

2. A window breaks down a long, dark street,
   And a siren wails in the night.
   But I'm alright 'cause I have you here with me,
   And I can almost see through the dark, there's a light.
   If you knew how much this moment means to me,
   And how long I've waited for your touch.
   If you knew how happy you are making me,
   I've never thought I'd love anyone so much.
   To Chorus

MIDNIGHT TRAIN TO GEORGIA

Words and Music by
JIM WEATHERLY

She kept   mine.

Yes, I'll be with her

I'M A BELIEVER

Words and Music by
NEIL DIAMOND

LOVE SONG

Words and Music by
LESLEY DUNCAN

Moderately

38

LOSING YOU

Words and Music by
RANDY NEWMAN

40

HALLELUJAH

Words and Music by
LEONARD COHEN

A SONG FOR YOU

Words and Music by
LEON RUSSELL

YESTERDAY

Words and Music by JOHN LENNON
and PAUL McCARTNEY

ok

58

LET IT BE ME
(Je T'appartiens)

English Words by MANN CURTIS
French Words by PIERRE DeLANOE
Music by GILBERT BECAUD

DESPERADO

Words and Music by DON HENLEY
and GLENN FREY

DON'T FORGET ME

Words and Music by
HARRY NILSSON

© 1974 (Renewed) GOLDEN SYRUP MUSIC
All Rights Administered by WARNER-TAMERLANE PUBLISHING CORP.
All Rights Reserved Used by Permission